MADE AT MIDNIGHT

ISAAC JILEN

Contents

Contents

Preface

"Made At Midnight" is a book of poetry, accumulation of some fortunate lines that came across the Author in his boring midnights. the content in the book is mainly fictious meant to be read with open mind and a love for poetry.

  "What will last, no one knows;
  Only Midnight can tell what tomorrow holds"
  Good Read ::

1. MIDNIGHT MOON

Blessing ray of moon;
On a bright spring night,
Loneliness got me soon;
Drove my sense left and right.

Searching for words in my mind;
To fill these fortunate lines,
Gazing at moon so beauty and kind;
Aroused the poet in me to shine.

Far above in the blue sky;
Yet, quenched my heart from dry,
Couldn't healed by anything worldly;
Found my peace in you, farly.

2. TOMORROW

The concept of tomorrow
Is that of a Weight, tilting between
Will it be,
Will it not be;
Tomorrow is not for you to wait
(Let's wait for tomorrow) No,
Tomorrow is the one that waits for you.
Will it be there for you?
Will it not be there for you?
For tomorrow is an everlasting concept
That will be there, even if you're not.

Tomorrow is mysterious yet certain.
An unspoken promise, that is
Kept and reneged at the same time,
A sign of hope,
A reason for hope,
A hope that drives people to live,
Live today to see the beautiful
Dawn of tomorrow.

3. TO YOUR ETERNITY

Let me cherish this moment
Before the goodbye steal our time;
For thou, are inconstant as comet,
Centuries will fly, finding your rime,
Might the demise find me, before
My gaze finds you again,
But my yearning for thee will implore
For millennials for thy beauty regain

Let me keep this moment frozen
For my conscious; to keep it's sane,
Let this depart mark my reign, over
Thy beauty and as thee lover.
Might I lose tranquillity in your goodbye;
Might the violent thought become my ally,
But my yearning for thee shall hold;
For millennials, until you're there for me to behold.

4. BIRD IN A CAGE

Methought, bird in a cage;
Constrained in the loop of life.
From afar, I held my gaze
Wonder if she dwells in her trife.

Methought, there'd be rage;
For she seemed to be in strife.
But my sight, just seen a page
Of her vast book, there I thrive.

Methought, she'd be a mage;
Seized my compassion, and my soul
Imprisoned in her charming maze.
For myself, I did enrol.

Methinks, She's a sage;
Charming like an angel, I parol.
Clasped in this moment of daze,
Will I find this moment's parole?

Methought, she's a bird in a cage,
Methinks, I'm the bird on her page.

5. BLISS I PLEA

Come forth, oh sorrow
Here's my portion, have it borrow
This sadness, that madness;
Push me into the blissful wilderness.

Over there lies my tomorrow
The path, all so narrow
Oh, what a mess, flowing less;
Rove me over to that happiness.

Come now, tomorrow to face
Warp me out of this phase;
Shoot shoot, I'm your arrow
So far, there- no more sorrow.

6. Stranger Of The Night

Hush, Stranger of my night
No more can take my might;
Harmonious slumber, you had swallow
Begging I, keep my sanity hollow

Hush, Stranger of my night
Quell deep, exempt my senses' sight;
No more, let my sanity glow,
Let it calm like a river flow.

How long, you'll have my Slumber blow
The night is old, leave me slow;
Bid me farewell of conscious fright,
Hush now, Stranger of my night.

The beating voice comes from below
O stranger: impeded thou, now I follow
The rhythmic voice in dreamy bright
Guiding the path to the drowsy light.
Be hush still, my stranger at night.

7. A WOMAN IN GALE

Oh, woman, that woman;
A kind, amongst many women.
An attire of cultural glow
Descending waist, like Siang she flows;

Orbiting around her body below
With the vibes of a traditional hello.
Covered in white with veins of black thread
Like a ruled page, her well-nurtured to be read.

The elegance of Gale, they're resplendent;
Halts everyone's gaze, as her attendant.
Apparel with numerous lore and tales
The essence of every tribal Female.

Oh, woman, that woman;
Covered in her glamorous 'Jese Kore'
With the Blessed beauty of 'Jimi Ane'
A grace of Dawn, alluring to every heart.

8. Castle Made Of Sand

The castle's made of sand,
Holding the heart that's on rage;
Crumbling, trembling it won't stand.

Holding on, they'll slip away from hand,
For no one can hold, the turning of page,
The castle's made of sand.

The glamour of men, in time will disband,
Shadow will tell, men have fallen prey to age,
Crumbling, trembling it won't stand.

Travel, rebel, make living a grand;
For the end, even meets the sage,
The castle's made of sand

Raging of the heart, will not withstand;
For judgement will set all ablaze,
Crumbling, trembling it won't stand

And the soul shall strive for land,
And the eyes in frozen state, after her last gaze.
The castle are made of sand.
Crumbling, trembling it won't stand.

9. Purple Before The Sun

Is that your hope or are you just bound;
Still holding on: facing the stratocumulus cloud,
The seabed howling of typhoon thread;
Announced to you juxtaposing the skies blue and red.

The purple-drawn sky howls your downfall;
The fall of hope and life, you'll recall.
Might as well be the glint before your dusk;
The dusk that shall conquer the purple clouds' husk.

Is that your hope: but hope never was so cunning,
Do not carve your sky of hope to be the purple of mourning;
Let this purple be your spring: the purple of Lilac,
Shimmering over the horizon, hosting the dawn of hope, back.

10. More Than Just A Friend

My love story with you
Is just a wish of mine;
Maybe it never occurred to you
But you're always on my mind.

Strange it is, that I fall;
Fall for you every time
But we know, we'll never call;
Call each other on love rhyme

Goodbye, to these feelings I harboured
It's our fate to not go beyond;
The friendship we've savoured.
Maybe, this is the end stage of our bond.

11. BEGGING I THEE

Let me build our tomorrow
With your joy, not the sorrow;
A design to expunge all our grief
Like the moment so brief. Dusk of relief.

Come, plunge into the future I've woven
With a thread of love and hope so even,
Be my sunshine in the autumn shade;
I'll be your shade, till summer fades.

Be my might like the summer light
Barren was my soul like a winter night
With you, what world that I cannot fight?
You're my sight in this darkness of bright.

Forever is not what I ask
Only before the soul leaves this husk;
What's left of our future, not the past
I know, nothing's ever built to last.

12. CHASING COLOURS

Let us call it Green,
To cheer our harmony that'll begin;
Love and serenity like nature that reign.
To the beginning of us, forever to be,
As a vigour for the future, that'll be heavy.
Let it be Green, not the Green of Envy.

Can we make it Pink,
Like the treasure, I'm laying out these inks;
Of this euphoria, always on the brink.
No, let's not make it humid;
Let it flow like a fluid, the broken were always rigid.
It should be pink of love, not the pink so timid

It should be Brown,
To hold us together till we're grown;
In comfort and honesty, we've drawn.
Drawing together the yet-to-come
White and blue, shall be in our dome;
Serving love, not avarice to succumb.

13. OUR GRAVEYARD

I plunged my heart into this sight
Scattered them over like debris
Not sure, how long can i keep this fight
My whole shattered in your demise

I'll keep hold of this life
Until there's a thought of you alive,
Piece by piece I'll knit my lies
Only truth shall be when with you I lie

Buried my being in this moment
To be with you in the darkness of other side;
Laying with you will be my hopes
Waiting for time, my living corpse

I shall beg all my peers
To put me right beside you, truly near;
"A grave shall consist of what is ours
I have always been one of hers"

14. CLOSING CURTAIN

Nurture me, O Nature
Or come give me your torture
I'm merely one of your creature.
Or come be my preacher.
Heal me of life's pressure
Mold me, hold me, be my teacher
Shower me love, like your sapphire.
All these worldly, against me they conspire;

Cold and grey became my feature
Closing in, my time in future
Hard, it's hard, laying on this stretcher
Counting on, my will on the brink of rupture
O mother, come witness my departure
O nature, in you, let me retire.

15. MINOR DOUBTS

How do I bend these thoughts
Haunting me, is all I know,
New is the spell, my psyche caught;
Heartache is all there now

Thought I'd grown used to it
The length between our lives;
There's love, I know I admit
But this is new, for you, I thrive.

We were meant to be, in this line
To feel love together but aching alone;
Every beat tells me, you are mine
Every breath asks, are you mine alone?

16. INTROSPECTION

What worth will my fight be
Shredding of thread is all I see,
Holding onto the knife, jabbing, swinging;
Own red dripping, how can it be?

Fighting is all I've done
Fought and fought, till I stood alone.
Wonder, where all my foes have gone,
Only the barren meadow in my front;

The moment I turn around, I see him running free
Like I've never won: even with my spree;
Cold gaze, raging eyes, Charging like he never lost
The enemy was always there, the enemy was always me

"Infinity is not enough for our fight;
Rise and charge, for no worth will you find"

17. Red Thread Of Fate

Gazing at the light of the night
Gray, the orb of light perceives;
Held out my palm, only red on sight
A waving cord the light conceives.

Thought, my sight had me deceive
An image of you had my mind freed;
Miles away in Siang does the light you receive
Shows the string: like the one I can read?

Might it be binding our fate, the Red Thread
Urges in you flowing through cold and hot,
My anguishes through Pare, surge over this dread;
In the calm, our aisle shall be, with an eternity knot.

The Red Thread, the path to the heart,
An oath of destiny to guide our part.

18. LOST BATTLE

No, this is not my true post
Fate severed me from my host:
The battle of life, I did lost
I'm an angel, not a ghost

I had the breath and the feel
The maker stole the land beneath my heel;
The battle of life, I did lost
I'm an angel, not a ghost

Maker summons me to the other side
The path seemed calm but its a tide
Of the wishes pulling me towards the living side.
Defied the summon, gave in to your urge,
But now I'm unworldly, waiting to be purged.
I did lose, the battle of life
But I'm an angel, hear my strife.

19. SOMEONE NOT ME

She will call him 'Love'
The one, who is your beloved;
Showering joy upon your world,
The one, who will be your mother's hope

He will call him 'Son'
Another height to your father's joy.
The bondage of brotherhood for
Your siblings to share.

Grateful he shall be
To be greeted by your world,
To be able to cherish you for life;
Living joy and anguish, you by his side.

Wish I had foreseen, this future
Where you are not mine, now I retire;
Yearning, one she calls 'love' was me;
One he calls 'son' was me;
The one who is 'him' was me.

20. Melancholy Of A Classroom

Yearning was all I have had
For a glimpse of my newly found lads;
Conjured for me, by the thread of fate.
The longing ended, I embraced you though late.

Every morn began, with joyful steps
The love, the joy, the fun, all for my keepsake;
The treasures, only for me, never to be shared;
Saved among the many, I have then fared.

I'm like the season, you shall bid Adieu
For our time, was meant to be in due
Like you, In Whoopee, many have passed
May you go on, and be the one among the mass.

Cherish my words, in your path of dwell to prevail;
With Hope and Joy, bidding Fare Thee Well.

21. THE FAIR LADY

She ain't no deity
But surely an angel.
Fairest among the creator's beauty,
Sparkled this gloaming heart
as if she a candle.

Gleaming flow of the blonde stream;
The golden crown of her glamour.
Might she be of another realm
Entered my heart's domain to
have my thoughts devour

Eyes as deep as the ocean;
Would draw any sailor closer to her.
The touch of eyes would froze me open,
She may be the Gorgon, petrifies my soul;
the price to be her beholder.

Walks the same path every light,
Thieviously, would I seek her sight
Might, she have perceived my eyes;

In my find, maybe, she discovered
my pain in her goodbyes.

22. A WOMAN

She is a mother and a sister
She is the symbol of creation
Presented by god to this barren world.
She is a daughter and a fighter
She is the heart of a loving family
And the balance between men and society.

She is the magnificence of nature;
She is as free as the birds
But her freedom is bound inside a cage.
She is praised by everyone;
She is never heard by anyone,
Deemed in society as second in sex.

She is the angel of her father
Kind and loving, graceful daughter
But never the same as her brother.
She is adored by the men
And cherished by the remain
But never the first in the lane.

She exists within a bound
That goes with her all around:
She is meant not to be confine
But to love and define:
As the bird with feather
Spreading her wings and flying higher and higher.

23. THE CAVE

A cave filled with knowledge,
Imparting among Crewmates;
The learned captain showering
The wisdom he has savoured;
Of many maps and journals
That led him to reach above.
Dozen of heads awaiting
Like an empty chest on hold;
Waiting for the lines, to be drawn
Some of gold, silver or more.
But the learned captain's insight
Doesn't fall equally for all;
One could fill only the right
Amount that each chest can hold.

One chest out of dozens
Filling not the line of gold
Nor of any pearl or jewel;
Rather, of the joyous voyage,
The learned captain won over
To draw the lines on the paper.

One chest out of dozen
Not filling gold nor silver,
But the insight of land and river
Across the cave of knowledge,
The sun, moon, stars and
the vast ocean, for him to discover.

24. UNWORTHY

Oh, what worth is my vision;
If my sight doesn't know your eyes,
Or If my glance doesn't show me the reason
Of you fading like the season.
Or did my eyes made the treason;
Blinded me in self-esteem prison.

Oh, what worth are my hands;
If my palm doesn't know your touch
Or if my touch can't perceive your face.
And what worth of my legs;
If my steps doesn't know your place
Or if my haste can't win over your farewell.

Oh, what worth are my lips;
If my smooch doesn't know your cheek
Or if my kiss can't touch your forehead.
And What worth of my heart;
If the beats doesn't know your name.
And of it's love, that couldn't keep you glad.

25. RUNNING IN CIRCLES

Treading on with the signs
Like the brown leaf on the sea;
Flowing further, losing all the green
And the fate as Humus with the grin

Flying away, among the wind
Like the ash gentle and light;
The blazing zeal gave up on the fight,
A conflagration, only a relic of mind.

Came distant from the dark
The sun, only a tip far apart;
Night hauls me, not the dawn art
The closer to the light, the heavier the darkness lurks.

26. A LOBOUR'S DAY

Off from home before dawn
Holding the spade, my weapon
Put up the smile, my face of clown
For my angel, joyous her day should go on

Arrived the first ray, Piercing my eyes
But boosted me up on my Shovel
Came the draining noon, my body sighs
Yet, can't rest arms; have to get home food avail.

Five on the clock, put down the materials
Tired, as if my body decayed
Relief came, time to see my Ariel
Heard her day went joyful, all my pain swayed

Forgot all the hardship, I'm in my base
To keep her happy, many times I'll put on my clown face

27. Stuck At The Moment

Stuck at the moment
Levitating on imagination.
Head full of dreams, but;
Body with no determination.
Many futures in thought;
No steps on the approach.

The older I become, darker it gets;
The vision of the future
Smaller and smaller it projects.
Yet, the whispering voice inside
Calls out to me and say;
Find yourself at the end of the maze.

28. GRAVEYARD

The fireflies twinkles;
Over my garden of love
So Beautifully,
Glowing, Glinting, they are
Sparkling over my love's graveyard

29. THE LAND

I'm on the ocean, floating.
Lost, tired and craving;
For the land above the blue
With the greenery of hope.
Not the tempting land
Deep below me, calling
Me to take my rest.

30. REMINISCENCE

And then nothing else mattered
After that soft touch of fate
My whole world began to fade
Under the dark sky of words uttered,
What is the price of my prayer?
All I hear are the words of betrayal
a warzone, the damage to collateral
The victim but unknown to the slayer,
Dreamer but of a broken dream
What's the broken dream anyway?
Can't it be inherited, another way
What's broken shouldn't be a Dream.
And then again, what of the broken?
The unmendable goblet that held the fire
The flame unravels, not in the choir
Mendable, but with scars as a token,
Touch? No, the stroke of fate
Swept away the hopeful green beneath
Ash? No, just fire without heat
Flew away from the palm, I did held late.

31. TIME WILL HEAL

They said the time will heal;
All these emotions of grieve
Which keeps me covered to thrive
For your hand, again I want to feel.
All these memories like a reel
As if you came back revive
From afterlife, back to me alive,
Just the hope, for this to be real.

You were claimed by The One,
To his arms, as if thou were Apostles
Holy and happy, to be in heaven.
For I shall, seek for new begun
Leaving past, opening new bottles;
So thou shall smile down, see'ng me leaven

32. ON THE SHORE OF TALO

Far apart, on a valley in the east;
Early glow shall be your sight,
Besides the beauty of flowing 'Talo';
The blessing stream of 'Masselo Zinu'

Amid the range of splendid flora
Heed to the lores of 'Ke-Meh-Ha';
With the tickiling of autumn sun
And the festive of 'Reh' on winter's hand.

You shall find her weaving 'Thunwe';
Drawn to the sorcery, everyone will be.
He will be rolling the knife; curvng bamboo
Forging the basket. beside him will be a glass of 'Yu'

Greet the sun goddess; rising above 'Sikang'
In her virgin ray; discover the heart of 'Dibang'

33. RECOLLECTION

Conjuring these thoughts;
To see it's worth,
Began from loving path
Reached the solitary spot,
Turned to a new chapter
Full of whispering voices,
Voices calling to find it;
Find the reason of everything,
But everything turn back
Back to the chapter it began;
The chapter said to be the best
That had already been laid to rest

34. TO GRANDMA

Longing on a lost
Couldn't really be easy.
To the sadness, I'm a host
When agony hit as a blitz

A wish for your return, now;
Is what I dream, I do.
Little that I know;
With dream come alive, comes nightmare too.

35. CAN I?

Can I have all the say?
So I can tell before I shy.
Let me now convey: before I lose my way,
The despair and sorrow I had to pay;

In your silence, I sensed my 'no'
The silence that once was a friend;
Came to me as 'Brute' guiding the end
Left me bleeding with daggers of your 'no'

Like a needle throbbing in my chest
Your words lanced on the crying east
Touched by the hands of shadow;
The grip incites a gloomy Meadow.

Can I have all the say?
So I can tell before I shy.
You are with me everywhere, every day;
Though in silence, I held you on in every word I pray.

36. CURE FOR ME

Is there any cure?
Cure from myself.
From my puzzled thoughts
That has drove me insane

Is there any cure?
Cure from myself.
From my unhealthy addiction
That has invaded my body

Is there any cure?
Cure from myself.
Maybe, I'm the cure myself;
Or am I the cause alone.

37. DREAM

Dreams can be many
Can be achieved by any

Dreams of people, always differ
It's your dream, so you must prefer

Dreams can never be shattered
It's your will to achieve, that retired

It is easier to have a dream
Harder to have it, redeemed

Your dream is meant to be achieved
Whether by you or someone else

38. LOVE CONDOLENCES

A wanderer in million of lives;
Took by fate; under your charm.
Seen million of faces;
Yours filled my defoilted heart.
Fell for thy kind nature;
Begged god, to hold your arm.
Season passed but not your charm;
Under that spell my heart is warm.
Scared of your no;
Kept my heart calm.
Never gave my love an allowance;
All that left is, my love condolence

39. *.*

A night of full moon
Beautiful and Nostalgic
Yet, it made me lonely;

We share the same moon
But not the moment,
It made me unhappy.

40. CLOSING STATEMENT

Oh bright light
Shine on me tonight
I've done my chores
And all my choirs
Putting my pen down
My mighty crown
Bleed my words
Rhyming those cords
Now, let me retire
In your beaming attire
Do shine me glory
I left out no worry
Rolled out my ink
Mind needs to sink
Closed lid tonight
Shine on me, oh bright light